THE LIBERATION OF EUROPE, 1944

BY

G.M.WILSON, CAPTAIN, THE 7th BN, THE GREEN HOWARDS REGT. (50th DIVN.)

Being a brief account of a few of the author's experiences on and subsequent to the 6th Day of June, 1944, in the greatest invasion by Land, Sea and Air, of all time.

CONTENTS

---FOREWORD ----

I must apologise in advance for the excess of
"ego" in this brief story - and at times for the bad
language - but it should be borne in mind that the
complete "original manuscript" consisted of a
letter written by me to my old friend Leslie
Hodge, whilst the War was still in progress, and
therefore was written "whilst the state of my mind
was unbalanced." The story is written entirely
from the point of view on the 7th Bn., the Green
Howards, from whose official war history (which
this is not) it can be seen that the Battalion has a
record which it will be difficult, if not impossible,
for another unit to surpass.
FEB., 1946.

Notes:1. Casualty figures are entirely approximate
   2. Dates, and even the sequence of events,
   are from memory only, and may be wrong.

DEDICATED TO THE MEMORY OF THE
OFFICERS AND MEN OF THE SEVENTH
BATTALION, THE GREEN HOWARDS, WHO
FELL IN THE CAMPAIGN DESCRIBED
HEREIN. THE P.B.I. WILL REMEMBER
THEM.

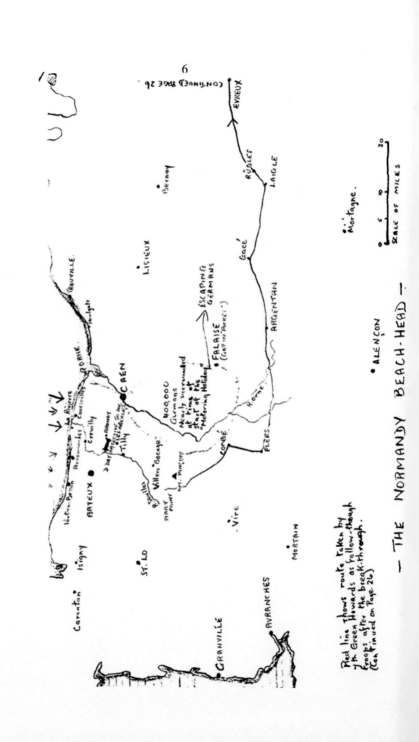

CONTINUED PAGE 26

6

— THE NORMANDY BEACH-HEAD —

PART ONE: THE LONG - AWAITED D-DAY

(1)

When would D-Day arrive? Would there be any invasion at all, or was it all a big bluff? Would bombing win the War and make an invasion unnecessary? What were we waiting for; had we still not enough men and equipment?

These were the types of questions the man in the street, the man in the Services, and the man in Occupied Europe, were asking from 1942 onwards.

We in the 50th (Northumbrian) Division did not know the answers until January 1944 whilst resting in England after the long and arduous tasks that had been allotted to us in the Middle East. It was then that we learned that in spite of other fully Invasion-trained Divisions who existed, the 50th was to make the assault. It was no surprise, therefore, for us to learn at the same time that General Montgomery (as he then was) had been brought home to take charge of the Expedition; for had he not said to us many a time "Wherever I go, there will the 50[th.] be found. "? Three years' training had to be crammed into four months, as the time decided upon was drawing nigh, and no doubt the powers that be had wind of the "V"weapons which made any delays suicidal. There were many rehearsals and finally the Dress Rehearsal, which many thought was the real thing, followed by the "briefing" of Officers, and sealing of the various camps.

It may be interesting to note some of the extraordinary detail which went to make up the preparations for the great event.

"Confucius he say - all eggs in same basket no good." Not a correct quotation, but it serves to introduce the principle we followed. It would be a most dangerous thing to allow the sinking of one boat to upset the plan of the Operation whether from a Division's point of view, or the lowly platoon. Thus, given so many assault craft, it had to be worked out who would travel in which boat, an R.V. being given on land where all would gather for reorganisation. The same thing happened on the big troopships which were to take us to within 7 miles of the enemy coast, so that only a small contingent of the Bn. was contained in any one troopship, and of these only a few went in each assault craft. In addition everything possible was done to duplicate things, especially the communications, which were bound to prove vital. This system was of course worked upon at the Rehearsals, so that by the time all was ready every Officer, N.C.O., and man knew which troopship and which assault craft he was to travel in, and the name of the person in charge, time of landing and where to R.V. on landing. What we did not know (except 2 Officers per Bn.) until we embarked was the correct names of the Places in Europe, and of the Day. But every soldier was put completely in the picture, and studied air photos, models etc., on the boat.

Such was the care taken that there were reinforcements for each particular job, waiting at the Embarkation Port in case of last minute illness or casualties! The location of the Rehearsal ground had been so carefully chosen that it bore a marked resemblance to the real spot, so with air photos as well, everyman knew what to expect and look for.

Water-proofing all vehicles and equipment had been no easy job, and had to be most carefully inspected before leaving, with the prospect of a six-foot depth on landing.

Thus it came about that I embarked at Southampton on the 2nd June, with thumping heart, and 48 hours' rations in my pack, to await "the beginning of the end. "

---

(2)

The place was La Rivierre - half way between Caen and Bayeux. The Day was 5th June. H Hour was 0700 - daylight. And we could not hope for much surprise in view of the huge preparations, large armada, preliminary bombing, and German spies. This was the information given us on the boat, a converted Liberty ship which looked as though it might fall to pieces any moment.

Hitch number one arrived on the evening of the 4th when we were informed by the ship's Captain that the weather had caused a postponement. We should either sail one day (24 Hrs.) late, or we should have to disembark into sealed camps and wait at least a fortnight; a decision would be made tomorrow. It certainly was pretty "choppy" now to say the least of it, and the ship was rolling very badly as we lay at anchor in the Solent. However the next morning, the speakers on the ship blared forth "Attention Everyone! All Officers will report to the Conference Room at once. Other Ranks stand by for an important announcement." And then we knew!

"Gentlemen. The Supreme Commander of the Operation, the details of which you already know, has decided that D Day is to be tomorrow 6th June, and H Hour 0700. He has taken this decision after consulting all his specialist advisers and in spite of a continued bad-weather forecast. You, your Country and the Free World have awaited this great day. Do your Duty, and may God be with you all! If you succeed - I am sorry - when you succeed, the end of this dreadful conflict will be in sight. Good luck!" It was the Captain, and there followed the final orders for the next morning. When my stomach had ceased to revolve, and I had pushed my heart back to its normal position from my mouth, I realised that this was "it".

---

(3)

We started off at dusk on the 5th, in the throes of a howling gale and I must say the sight of the rest of our convoy seemed most disappointing. Sicily had shown an immense display of sea-might and now all I saw was, perhaps twelve troop ships, a few tank landing craft, and a destroyer or two. However, I supposed "they" knew what they were doing, as of course they did.

Dinner that night was not a pleasant meal. Not that there was the same discordant atmosphere that one comes to expect of Charles Laughton's ships. Nevertheless, conversation was a little difficult, and the suet pudding was inclined to stick in one's throat, or so I found.
And so to bed - a wooden bench with one blanket and no mattress, and a gnawing fear of the morrow ... 23 ... 2359 ... 0100 ... 0200 ... sleep was not terribly easy. Perhaps we had better pray ...... for once. "God, save me" ....no that won't do; must put up a show ... "God, help me to suffer in silence, and may we be successful." How's that? What's that? Good heavens, Reveille! 0330 ... June 6th, 1944 ... 0330 .... JUNE 6th.

(4)

Well, "Dwight" had taken the plunge, and so did we, very nearly. As I have said, we were first "in" and as we got off the big boats into the little-uns, we nearly had it. Landing craft do not stand much buffeting about and here was a sea such as would make even a good sailor think twice! Then they got the rope which lowered us down (I fear I am no good at nautical terms) entangled somewhere and it took 27 minutes to get it right, every one of which nearly saw us overturn. It was quite bloody, and we had seven miles or so to do at 3 - 4 miles an hour, and all the time the certainty in one's mind that we must either go down, or meet our doom on the beaches we had dreamed about for months. It would be no picnic like the Sicily landing, that we knew. But we had at least expected a fairly calm sea in which to do or die.

But I digress. I had refused the sea-sickness tablets on principle as a good sailor should and it amused me greatly to see the faces of all present in my craft - about 24 people, including the Commanding Officer - gradually turn green till they dashed one by one to the side of the craft!

.... What a stupid lot ... no guts, that's what it is ... not one left fit to fight, except me ... I wonder what I look like? .... feel O.K. ... God, this wind! ... That's right, bring it up ... Have you got through on that Wireless? Can't stop the Invasion for a bit of sea-sickness, you know ... ugh, what a colour .... don't seem to be getting any nearer the coast; must be nearly, good Lord it's a quarter to seven now: we'll be late ... There go the big guns, must be at least 16 inch ... Heavens, this sea ... There goes one of those bloody rocket craft they told us about, what a din ...What did they say, 500 rockets per boat in 3 minutes on to an area of 200 square yards? ... or was it 300? ...... Does it matter? ... Phew, it's rough ... keep trying to get through Signaller, you can be ill in between ... don't they all look bloody ill .... wonder what is waiting on that blasted beach ... not much I hope after those rockets ... and bombers ... and Typhoons ... Just Spandaus and Mortars I suppose ... funny, feel a bit queer myself ... are we getting any nearer; I suppose a bit ... look at those water spouts - or are they shells? Must be I suppose. Christ, I feel frightful ... shouldn't have had that rum .... and so on until yes, I really was sick for the first time, though I still swear it was more the nervous tension than the sea. And anyway, I was the last to fall!

———

(5)

Came the Beach! The view was rather different from that of the previous night in the Solent. As far as the eye could see in both directions, small craft of all types were being buffeted towards the coast along which at various points we could see the enemy opening fire. Back behind us were the troopships awaiting the return on the landing craft to pick up the second wave of troops. Innumerable war-ships of all types were pounding the coast and inland strong-points with their big guns, and the air was alive with aircraft, but without any swastikas and white crosses. After the rope trouble our boat was rather behind schedule and we knew from the Wireless that most of our Coys. were ashore. There were some nasty poles sticking out of the water by the beach (some of which were being dealt with by the now-famous Frogmen, who had travelled on our troopship and left half an hour earlier) and these poles had mines of various types fixed on top so as to detonate at a touch. There was only just room to get between these mines and with the rough sea, craft were hitting them all along the beach, though casualties caused were fairly light as the men were near enough to the shore to wade or swim in.

Luckily (we could scarcely believe it) there was very little fire coming from our immediate front though numerous battles had flared up all along the beaches on either side of us. Actually, at the time we scarcely noticed this lack of fire, so anxious were we to touch terra firma, if we could only miss the mines. We arrived at these dreaded obstacles, and the swell seemed worse than ever. By some cool and brilliant seamanship the Craft Skipper, a lad of 20, "made it" and we were through.

It merely (!) remained to jump off into four feet of water and wade ashore, a task none too easy in full kit. It rather reminded me of surf bathing in North Cornwall, though I would not say it was quite so enjoyable as that popular pastime. In getting ashore I slipped on a small rock, and fell onto a mined pole. Either it was a dud, or else the frogmen had saved my life, as all I received was a cut in the hand from a completely dead mine of the Teller family.

I was on French Soil!

_____
(6)

Now let me see, what did I usually do on landing in France? A nice Estaminet? Good heavens! Of course, there's a job in hand.

Our task for D Day, so often rehearsed, so often debated upon, so often dreamt about, was to clear the beaches and proceed as far as (i) the main road Bayeux to Caen and (ii) the Railway Brest - Paris parallel to the road, about 7 - 8 miles inland.

The next spot of bother came when I realised that my two alternative wireless links to Brigade were missing. The big "half-track" truck had apparently failed to get ashore and the signaller with the second set in a hand-cart, was nowhere to be seen. Furthermore, we discovered that we had been landed a mile away from the correct beach. It turned out afterwards that this had been done on purpose as a bloody battle was in progress on our own beach.

Stepping rapidly over a number of bodies and wounded - mainly our own, as such enemy who were not now prisoners, had been blown to the four winds by the preliminary bombardment - I made my way with our boat-party towards our R.V., a walk, as I have said of about a mile. We kept to the beach (which appeared unmined) for fear of mines and it was very heavy going in soaking clothes and heavy equipment. Luckily things were pretty quiet now except for occasional mortaring and the constant whine of our big naval shells going overhead to their "switch" targets inland.   The secret "DD" tanks which had "swum" in, had been a great success and were busy getting rid of their swim-suits preparatory to supporting us. It was very encouraging to see them safely ashore, as on rehearsals they had been a flop; we later learned it was because to preserve the secret the real ones had not been used, but some early experimental tanks.

The first job was to collect together the various men who, it will be remembered, had

travelled piecemeal. One by one they filtered
in, and again luck was with me - I had not lost
a single man! I sat there scarcely believing it,
when I was brought to my senses by a burst of
spandau fire which plunged into the bank a
few yards away. There was little cover where
we were so we instinctively dashed for the
other side of the road where a brick wall
would at least cover us from view, if not from
bullets. There was only one answer in
moving about ... risk it. For we knew from air
photos that the whole area was stiff with mines
(the disturbed earth showed up clearly on these
remarkable R.A.F. aids) but if one was to
move carefully each time, we should have
covered no ground at all, and in this particular
instance, we should all have received a
bellyful of lead.

It now dawned on me that in the
excitement of everything I was failing
miserably to execute the job in hand -
communications. If we were to stand a dog's
chance, it was essential to let Brigade (who
were still on the water) know the position, and
bloody quickly at that. Failing information,
they would assume we had failed and would
land the next wave elsewhere, it being an

Army "sine qua non" not to reinforce failure, only success. The Company sets back to me were working fairly well, so we knew how things were going with them; they had taken the first objective, some big guns a few hundred yards inland, in various directions. All but one battery had been knocked out by the R.A.F. early that morning, and this one contained 40 - 50 very bomb-happy Germans who failed to fire a shot. So far so good, if the news could be got to Brigade.

I was just despairing, when the "hand-cart" alternative wireless came into sight and in no time the vital news was through.

---

(7)

During our careful study of the enemy layout, we had been told that once we had cleared the beach area, there would be nothing to stop us up to the final objective, except for mines and a fortified farmhouse some 6 miles inland. This was of course working on the assumption that Gerry was not awaiting us in unexpected strength. However, the security side of things must have been amazingly good, because they certainly did not expect us, at any rate on our front. In actual fact, where the

Americans landed further South the Bosche
had only just finished an anti-invasion
Exercise and had expected nothing - perhaps
because of the dreadful weather. The
Exercise, of course, was a bit of bad luck for
our Allies, as it meant there was a large
concentration of troops in the vicinity, and
their landing was very costly.

The forecast on our strip was very
correct, as except for a few snipers we had no
trouble for some five miles. Soon after we
had set off we met our first civilians and the
reception we received is perhaps worth
recording. They must have been either bomb-
happy or pro-German because we were mostly
received with cold stares and stony silence,
and this attitude persisted throughout our long
stay in Normandy. Some, admittedly, seemed
mildly pleased and brought out some frightful
cider to quench our thirsts, and some few
waved to us. It should be said in all fairness,
however, that not only are these people of a
dour and quiet nature, but most of them had
lost relations in the bombing and fighting and
had had their homes destroyed, and often
livelihood ruined. This would not make for a
great welcome, neither would the fact that the

Germans (as we learned later) had not interfered with their lives to any great extent. Still, the reception was to us, at the time, very disappointing after what we had conceitedly expected.

So things were going very much to plan, if a little late owing to the weather and the fact that we had landed at the wrong place. Here we were, a few miles inland and with remarkably few casualties.

I think I was dreaming about our amazing luck at this very moment, but in any case I was soon brought down to earth (literally!) by the unmistakable crack of an 88 m.m. (the finest gun of its type in the world, and the terror of all tank crews from desert days) just ahead of us.   Yes, three Shermans - the ones I had seen on the beach - who were supporting us, were blazing merrily in the low ground ahead and it was obvious we had bumped something. It was no doubt the "fortified farm" we had expected.

It was now almost dusk and most of us were just about "all in" after a tiring day, both mentally and physically and we were

wondering how we were to hope to capture the
farm in this condition, when the Brigadier
ordered us to laager for the night, about two
miles short of our objectives.   The reason
for this change in the orders, we learned, was
that we were the only Brigade to get as far
inland on the whole invasion coast, and in fact
fighting was still going on along the beaches in
many areas. A deep, thinly held, salient
would have been too risky. We dug in, and
those who were lucky enough not to be on
Guard or on Duty tried - without much
difficulty - to get some sleep.

------

(8)

And that was D Day! Looking back on
it afterwards, I have little hesitation in saying
it was just about the easiest day we had, in
contact with the enemy, in that whole six
months stay in Europe.   How the casualties in
the Battalion were kept so low - about 20 - it is
impossible to say, but the deaths and injuries
from the dreaded network of mines which we
knew existed in millions was - NIL.

Come what may, we at least had a foothold.

PART II - THE BEACH - HEAD: 1914 AGAIN

(1)

The Second World War produced many Operations in which there were either Beach-heads or Bridgeheads the latter being the expression used when it is a River or Lake concerned instead of Sea. All of these to date had proved most unpleasant, though often the early stages had been fairly easy. Wadi Akarit, Sicily, Salerno, Anzio are just a few and any man who has lived through one of these episodes will know just how unpleasant they can be. There are many troops in a small area under constant bombardment and the ultimate object of the effecting of a break-out is always a matter of time. Our friend the Normandy Beach-head was no exception and was "the beach-head to end all beach-heads" - though it did not do so.

---

(2)

We were off again at 0500 on the 7th June with the object of reaching the previous day's objectives. The "farm" proved quite troublesome, but fell to us after a three-hours fight. How the place was captured for the loss of a handful of men I shall never understand.

We found afterwards that the area of about 3 acres was beautifully defended. The living and working accommodation was not in the farm, which we had laid in ruins, but in cunningly concealed huts in the trees a few hundred yards away. They contained much undamaged and valuable Radio equipment, as the station was engaged in Radio-location work. The area was a network of very deep trenches and dug-outs and commanded a grand field of fire all round the compass.

Carefully sighted machine and anti-tank guns gave the Air Force personnel (some 80 bodies) defending it every opportunity of inflicting colossal slaughter on us, and of course in addition the surrounding ground was heavily mined. However, our previous experience of such attacks stood us in good stead and the enemy were in our hands soon after what would have been breakfast time.

Leaving a party at the Farm, the Battalion proceeded without further opposition to take up positions on the high ground overlooking the Railway, and the main Caen - Bayeux Road was in our hands. I say overlooking, but this is not the right word as we were now entering the Bocage country, and there were dense forests and tall grass everywhere, making the railway more or less invisible, and incidentally making the progress most difficult and dangerous. Here we parked, to await further orders, and used the time digging in, cleaning up, and getting some much-needed rest.   The "Farm" proved an excellent Road-House to us, being full of German food and wine and much loot was obtained.

---

(3)

All of the landings succeeded and in a few days the Army Group had a pretty good strip up to 10 or 15 miles inland for a considerable way.   Priority one now was to obtain a Port (Brest or Le Havre) though we knew that the now famous Mulberry would be all right in an emergency. However, these were tasks for other units and did not directly concern us.   We still awaited orders; we got a little rest, the wireless half-track came up, having managed to get ashore, and things all round looked pretty bright. A sister Brigade had captured Bayeux intact without much trouble, and there was still no sign of the

Luftwaffe, though a few planes were bombing the beaches each night.

It had been forecast to us that the enemy mobile reserve (his main strength) could not strike for 48 hours, and then it was unlikely to come against our sector, though local counter-attacks were inevitable at any time. This information proved (as usual) correct.

The expected counter-attacks developed but were held easily enough as there was no sign yet of Artillery or tanks. Much probing by our own armour and recce units was going on but there seemed no sign of any move forward. We often had the eerie experience of getting the spent solid shots from a tank battle away to the flank whistling slowly (really slowly) through the air and coming to ground with a thud. After seven or eight days of intensive patrolling, we were relieved by a Division fresh from England (the third British Division to land, 3rd Div. having assaulted with us) and it rather seemed to bear out what we had been told during training: "Those who survive the landing will not be in for long, but will be pulled out for re-fitting." They put us for our "rest" in the same field as the Heavy

Artillery, and sure enough the following morning we received fresh orders for battle, and our hopes were dashed to the ground. We were to try and probe forward on a sector right of where the fortified farm was, in the hope of getting to the aid of the Desert Rats (7th Armoured Division) who had pushed right inland to Villers Bocage (on the Cherbourg - Caen Road) on D+1 but had met heavy Armoured opposition and were more or less surrounded.

---

(4)

We very soon bumped opposition of unknown strength and after a few miles were held up - after losing several very good officers and men - near a tiny village called Les Oreilles. The outcome was that in spite of numerous attacks all along this sector by the various units, no headway was made and it was in this area that we had to remain until shortly before the breakthrough by the Americans. It was of course, in many ways, 1914 all over again, and most people know how deadly that was. How our fathers stuck it for four years I cannot imagine; and of course in this warfare, one Arm suffers misery, filth, casualties more than its supporting Arms have ever dreamed of - the Poor Bloody Infantry.

It was not long before bodies (human and Bovine) began to pile up, producing the overbearing stench of death, and the early optimism began to give way to a feeling of impatience at the slow progress.

Most factors went against the Allies at this time. The weather - never very good since June 3rd! - turned very wet, and the continued gales greatly hampered the great build-up of men and supplies. Days, and sometimes weeks, went by without a man being landed. The commitments at Caen, where the bulk of the British and Canadian strength was forgathering, did not allow our sector any reliefs and during the whole period there was absolutely nothing between our "thin red line" and the coast. We realised that we were the buffer between two great and ever increasing Armies and knew that the big plan was to be either - 1. The British Armies to attract the main enemy strength to Caen, and thus allow the Yanks a comparatively easy breakout or 2. If the Bosche concentrated on the Yanks who were South of

us, then the British could break out at Caen
and make for the tank country ahead.

I believe the High Command hoped for
the first alternative, because the British troops
were known to be best for dogged "hanging-
on" against great odds, whilst the Yanks were
(it was believed) past masters at fast-moving
warfare.

Be that as it may, it was number one
alternative that occurred. The famous feint at
Caen was put in, and but for the weather
breaking at a vital moment, might have even
turned into a break-through. However, the
main object of drawing nearly all German
strength was accomplished - to the detriment
of many good men in Britain and Canada's
tiny armies - and of course the Americans
were through in no time.

This is no part of this account, and
merely serves to show that at this stage we had
a minor (but nonetheless bloody) role. We had
not the strength of arms to advance but were
able (often with difficulty in the face of great
tank onslaughts) to hold our ground, and keep
the enemy wondering.

(5)

Though there were several lateral changes round of units throughout our stay in this hateful area, on only two occasions after the initial attack was forward progress made.

The first occurred early on (about D+8 or 9, I should say) when we were ordered to push on from Les Oreilles after the initial hold-up. All Companies reached their day's objectives at about dusk, very tired and hungry. Before they could dig in, however, the two forward Companies were strongly counter-attacked by Tiger tanks. Although one was left burning after a PIAT hit, the poor wretches of course stood no chance above ground, and though the Commanding Officer personally supervised the fighting, one Company were soon all killed or captured and the C.O. was also taken prisoner; he escaped a day or so later. The remainder of the Battalion, to save being over-run (we had no tank support, and little in the anti-tank line) withdrew back to the reserve battalion half a mile behind, where the line was held. It was a nasty shaking-up, with over 100 casualties, and we needed considerable re-organising -

and a new C.O. . What really happened was "the mixture as before". The Bosche practically always held a series of positions thinly with spandau machine-guns and then if the positions were captured, his main force (with tanks) some 400-800 yds in rear immediately counter-attacked before their opponents were organised. We always knew it would happen but were rather powerless to find a suitable antidote.

The other occasion was some 18 days later, when another advance was ordered, again with our Battalion in the van. A similar thing happened except that this time we held on, in spite of the worst mortaring and shelling we had yet experienced. The casualty list was again heavy, and the total dead and wounded was now rising alarmingly with little to show - as occurred so often in the last War. We were still only about two miles from Les Oreilles and another attempt to advance in the very close country met with no success.

It was about this time that the R.A.F. sent over 500 heavies at dusk one day to bomb Villers Bocage to oblivion, in order to assist the still beleaguered Desert Rats. It was a sight I shall never forget; it reminded me of a propaganda film and was almost laughable in its massiveness, and seemed to us to be the beginning of the end, though in actual fact the effect it had on the course of events was pretty small. However, it must have helped the Armour a certain amount, if it did not save the lives of those inhabitants who had ignored our warning leaflets a few hours before.

The feeling of us all towards the end of this bad period is to some extent summed up in a "Western Brothers" song which I wrote in a rest camp on the coast which 30 Corps had the foresight to start, and to which we were sent in turn for 48 hours. This composition is reproduced at the end of this account.

---

(6)

Our first full-scale rest came at last - somewhere around D+50. It took place near Bayeux (a dirty town, and with little or nothing to sell in the way of food and drink, and no entertainment) and lasted 5 days, during which time we had a good clean up and rest.

Whilst here, we learned of the great American attacks in the South-West which were to precede their break-through, and we were ordered to try yet again to get to Villers Bocage, but this time via the dominating feature of all Normandy, Mont Pinçon, which had been captured at great cost only that same morning by a sister Division of 30 Corps.   In fact, the whole Front had flared up again, and if five days had not put us in fine fettle, at least things appeared to be on the move at last.

Some of the details of this latest operation and its immediate successor for Saint Pierre la Vielle may be worth recording, in that it was the most unpleasant battle we had had up to this time - in other words in the whole Normandy Campaign.

We sent off an advance party to contact the units on the Mont and the rest followed on foot, except for the carriers, guns and H.Q. vehicles. The roads were terribly congested as we passed through scores of ruined villages, the roadside littered with British and German crosses. Luckily, it was still quite an occasion if even one Bosche plane appeared so that there was not a lot to worry about in regard to straffing..

This was not a good day for the wireless sets, so that it follows almost automatically that it was a bad day for the battle. There was much confusion, a very great amount of enemy shelling and mortaring, and a good supply of 88 m.m. guns to catch the unwary tank or vehicle. We had not reached the objective, about 4 miles past Mt. Pinçon along the Villers Road, by nightfall, and the ordered Night advance to complete things was little short of chaotic. Inter-Brigade liaison was poor and no-one quite knew who was where.

In spite of all, the objective was taken and whilst digging-in proceeded, the Bn. Pioneers were busy preparing another good supply of crosses for the use of the burial parties. It was the Battalion wit who told the Pioneers the names of the fallen, and he strongly recommended them to obtain a nominal roll from the Orderly Room so that they could make out a cross for everyone including themselves, in advance!

For once no counter-attack developed, though shelling went on for the two days we awaited further orders. When these orders came we proceeded to St. Pierre, on a dominating hill about two miles from the elusive Villers Bocage, and which village the tired but still game troops took in great style, finishing with our best bag of prisoners to date - 150.

Never make the mistake of capturing an enemy position and taking over the same position. You will be blasted without respite; we found that out here, though we were lucky with casualties. In the morning all was dead quiet and we were able to clear up the area, which was littered with dead. We had the "pleasure" of encountering the German at his worst, as they had taken pains to booby- trap two of their own bodies.

The quiet continued, and we marched into Villers Bocage without opposition, amidst great evidence of the dreadful battle the Desert Rats had endured. We could scarcely tell where the town had been as the R.A.F. raid had not left a single brick standing; the position of the Roads could barely be determined, and Gerry had made no effort to clear the debris.

_____
(7)

The Corps Commander came to see us the next day, and thanked us for all we had done. Sixty German Divisions were in full flight, being very heavily pounded from the air, day and night. It was August 17th, 1944.

The Battle of Normandy was won!

PART III: THE BREAKTHROUGH IN NORMANDY

(1)

The great news given to us by the General was followed by some details of our rôle in the immediate future. It was part of a new organisation at the highest level. The big plan was, as is now common knowledge, for a huge sweep inland by the Americans in the hope of surrounding the remaining and disorganised Germans, rather than an immediate dash to Paris. If the Bosche broke out of this steel ring, another great sweep would be made; and so on. These tactics were at this moment proceeding, and the first great surrounding movement was almost complete, but there was a narrow gap near Falaise which the enemy were fighting tooth and nail to keep open; many in fact did escape, though the carnage all this time was colossal and the roads were littered even worse than they had been in the great North African rout of Rommel.

This was the picture when we had received our new orders. We were to become a "follow-through" Division; an Infantry Mobile Division following the Armour in a

THE "MOTORING HOLIDAY"
AUGUST, 1944.

great dash across occupied France and Belgium. Or, as the General put it "the long awaited motoring holiday has arrived; go and enjoy it." The transport arrived in large numbers forthwith (such was the magnificent organisation of the whole campaign) and we went and enjoyed it.

===============
(2)

To the weary, almost dispirited, bomb-happy troops, no greater tonic could have been given. We spent many long days dashing across the countryside just as though we had been on ...... well a motoring holiday. Far from mild was the reception given us now, and every town and village, however small, turned out to a man to form a seething, cheering mob, and it rather made one's throat lumpy to see the spontaneous look of gratitude on the faces of the population after five years of slavery. Wine was terribly scarce, but that did not prevent these people from bringing out the small amount they had hidden from the Bosche, for the benefit of the ever-thirsty Tommy. Often it was difficult to make progress through these crowds, and a tin hat was essential if one was to avoid being hit by the apples, pears, tomatoes and other edibles which were thrown into our vehicles.

Of course the Maquis were very eager to help (and at times did) but they were rather inclined to make unnecessary remarks such as "the enemy left this morning", "the War is over", "I know where a Bosche was hiding last week" and so on. With their scarcity of transport they were quite out of the latest picture, but only naturally wanted to let us know that they existed and were right on the job.

Of course, the nights were a disgrace, and the celebration that went on was nobody's business, though we did not have to worry about the troops being ready for the 0530 set-off - they were not going to miss it for all the coal in Newcastle.

Twenty miles today, forty tomorrow, a hold-up whilst Yanks and British argued as to who should go first, and so the mad dash continued, with no sign of a battered enemy. Condé, Flers, River Orne, Argentan - a very battered town when we arrived, after a bitter battle over the great pocket - Gacé, Laigle, Rûgles. Here we halted for 24 hours whilst the Armour pushed on; a pretty little village with a remarkably good public baths, of which we made good use, and incidentally some excellent champagne. On again through cheering Evereux, Pacy, to the Seine. The Allies were almost in Paris and two almost unopposed crossings had been made opposite us at Vernon and Mantes. Further downstream still, the escaping Bosches were being pounded all the time and the bloodshed must have been frightful. Over the River we went at Gasny, and another triumphant day was over. What a lovely war!

---

(3)

The daily mileage was getting bigger now, and remember, thirty miles may not seem a lot but it is when the roads are crammed for hundreds of miles with the transport of several divisions - of different nationalities and with bridges blown to hold up the proceedings. Petrol was no worry yet, as we had aboard enough for 250 miles, and in any case supplies were following up. There was only one order: speed, speed and more speed.

Beauvais, Amiens (in ruins from, I think, 1940) and Albert, famous in the 1914-18 War and now an S.S. stronghold.

I do not like Germans - at least during war time - and I perfectly loathe Nazis, but when it comes to S.S. Troops it is the end. Arrogant, unbelievably cruel, fanatical and pretty well inhuman: not very nice to know.

We had forgotten a war was on and now here we were again. The locals in the previous village had told us the town was still occupied and we were ordered to take the place by evening - it was then 1530. It was dark before we reached the outskirts but patrols (that inevitable stand-by, poor devils) went on. Groping around a medium sized town in pitch black with a wildly excited population all trying to point out the Bosche strong-points in rapid French, is no easy matter and no main contact was made. The Carrier platoon - brave lads all, who had done sterling work throughout, with their flimsy armoured vehicles - who had been sent to a flank to cut off the enemy retreat, had more success however. They opened fire on the fleeing bullies and caused great havoc. The next day we marched in to Albert without opposition, and with a great bag of prisoners who were by now pretty cowed.

We were invited into the Town Hall, an immense building of typical French style, where we set up H.Q., posting the Companies on the various exit roads, pending further orders. The town and its wife turned up in strength and most of the morning was spent watching prisoners and collaborators being brought through the crowds to the Town Hall, amidst great booing. The latter were stood on the steps to receive judgement from the people. If they booed they were clamped into gaol, and in the case of women, had their hair shaved completely off there and then, in public. Really well known cases were taken round the back and shot at once.

Meantime, the celebration was going apace, alcoholically speaking, and it was with great difficulty that the Battalion was "rounded up" when orders to move on were received at lunch time. Au revoir to Albert!

---

(4)
Famous names of the First World War
continued to crop up on our Route. Bapaume,
Arras, Douais, and so across the border into
Belgium; we did not wait for the customs as
we had an awful lot to declare, but dashed on
to Tournai, a bigger town than would appear
from the average map. We installed ourselves
in the best hotel, which reeked as only
Germans can, and learned we were to stay for
a while to deal with the many "pockets" which
had been left behind in our great dash. So
whilst others continued the chase, we set about
gathering in the enemy. A pleasant and most
hospitable people inhabit this town and we
received co-operation wherever we went. In a
few days our bag of prisoners was over 5,000,
almost without a shot being fired. We laughed
over one German Colonel who telephoned (!)
us from 20 miles up the road and said he was
prepared to surrender his battalion intact if we
would send out transport for them! We called
him a pig-dog and said he must walk, but he
pleaded their boots were all worn out, and
failing transport they would stand and fight.
Ever merciful, and not requiring unnecessary
casualties (heaven knows they had been heavy
enough in Normandy - perhaps 500 out of 800)

we obliged and sure enough there they were lined up on parade, and on sight of the trucks a great cheer went up .... the dirty parasites. I wondered if our lads would have got transport from the Bosche in similar circumstances.

After some days - almost a week - fresh orders came through for us to join the Division who had been doing similar work at Alost and Brussels, so we continued the motoring.

----

(5)

Not only were we to move on, but we were to do the maximum possible mileage with a limit of Albert Canal which it was believed might be held.

We did the maximum possible - and reached Albert Canal when the speedometers showed 118 miles for the one day, surely a record. At the large town of Malines we received the best reception of all, and in addition to the usual fruit and vegetables, we were given enormous quantities of - oh! forbidden fruit - ICE CREAM. A very decent looking place, one way and another, and we wished we could have stayed. One woman,

possibly English, shouted in Gracie Fields
dialect: "Gradely dun, lads, tha's nearly wun!"

It was amusing to us at the time to hear
the locals cry in broken English (no French
here, only Flemish) "Good bye, Tommy"
which we correctly assumed meant "Hullo,
Tommy." But the joke of it all was that it was
"Good bye, Tommy" in another few miles,
when we discovered at the Canal that it was
held, and held in strength!
Good bye, my foot!

PART IV. THE ALBERT CANAL: BOSCHE AGAIN

(1)

Military Training Pamphlets state in great glee that for a river crossing a platoon gets (as far as I remember) one or perhaps two assault boats. Our brigade received their orders that night - we had arrived at the Canal at dusk - which were to cross and make a bridgehead during the night. For this purpose were allotted two ramshackle assault boats - for the Brigade!

The canal at this point (see map, page 55) is absolutely dead straight as far as the eye can see, in both directions. Both banks were completely without cover, except that at the spot chosen there was a very shallow hollow in the North bank. There was also a blown bridge some 200 yards West along the canal. The North bank was lined in good strength by G.H.F. personnel reinforced by anyone else available. The plan was for 151 Bde. to cross further East - objective Gheel, a small town on the "Island" between the canal and the next barrier, the Meuse - Escaut Canal, about 5 miles away. Our Bde., 69th, was to form a different bridgehead to (a) help 151 by drawing enemy from Gheel and (b) ultimately join up with 151. The object of the Operation was, briefly, to outflank Antwerp in which fighting was already going on, and which would be a very vital port if progress to Germany was to be continued. The supplies at the moment still had to come from the Original French Ports - such few of them as had been captured.

Such was the general layout.

––––––––––––––––
(2)

A sister Battalion made the crossing, so I cannot give any information about this, except that they "made it" after much fighting and heavy casualties, and formed a small bridgehead not more than a few hundred yards square. Now came our turn (the same night, though we were very tired from our long day's journey from Tournai) and most Coys crossed without serious incident. Towards the end of the night the sappers had completed an excellent job under heavy fire in knocking together a raft big enough to hold a small vehicle, and some 30 men. This they solemnly pulled backwards and forwards for about 36 hours. I tried it myself, and cannot understand how they managed it, and in the end they mostly passed out from sheer exhaustion - those who survived the shelling.

We were over, and bore off Westwards to enlarge the bridgehead, which was, however, still only about 300 yards deep, i.e. away from the Canal. We heard bloody fighting going on at Gheel, where fires lit up the whole countryside, and received word that the Durhams of 151 Bde. were having a rough time. Shelling, mortaring, and counter-attacks were all more or less perpetually going on, but we held our ground, and the next evening we received orders to extend the bridge-head northwards for about a mile.

The troops were a little "browned off" by now, and as we moved forward in the pitch blackness, the noise made was quite incredible. Drinking mugs, spades, shovels, rifles and equipment joined with the voices of men in creating quite an orchestral concert. Nothing happened, however, and the allotted positions were reached without mishap; noisy digging in commenced, and came the dawn. It was not long before things began to happen all round and numerous close-quarter fighting ensued in which part of Bn. H.Q. had to fight for its very life. Luckily, the Bosche were braver than they were clever, and soon the whole sortie was dead or taken prisoner, with few casualties to us. It was only then we learned that we had passed right through their positions the previous night, but all including sentries were so drunk on local hooch that they had heard nothing. In the morning they saw us in their rear and decided to attack us; there were about 100 all told, and had they been alert, could have given us much trouble that night.

---

(3)

It is not possible to hand over to another unit in the middle of a battle, and our experiences in this connection are noted in the next little incident. The counter-attacking by Gerry continued several times a day for the next 3 days, all attacks being safely held. Then we were told that other big plans were afoot and that we were to return to our rôle of follow-through troops, which looked good enough to us; certainly not worth arguing about ! The advance party of a battalion from the 15th Scottish Division arrived early in the morning and the main body began to trickle over the canal by the Bailey Bridge which the sappers had built, at about 1100 hrs. Wham! It started.

Gerry had gathered all his remaining forces together for a final crack at us, with plenty of tank and artillery support, and just as the C.O. was saying to the Scottish, "O.K., your chaps may as well start coming in." all hell was let loose.

The battle raged with the utmost ferocity for 8 hours and at times the news put through by wireless by Companies was not very reassuring. One Company were partly over-run and surrounded by several heavy tanks and to show the difficulty of knocking out a Tiger let me say that one of our 6 pounders, firing partly normal solid shot and partly "Sabre" special ammunition hit one over twenty times before it was put out of commission. Things were grim, and each of the three forward Companies in turn got into difficulties. Brigade were asked for help and they agreed to despatch a troop of Shermans at once.

Meantime the Scots were told to lay low at the bridge as they were not sufficiently in the picture to be of much help at the moment. All members of their advance party became casualties to make matters worse, so they would not have known where to go.

Hay-stacks and cottages were going up in flames all over the place and it really looked as though we would be hard put to hold out. When a German soldier of the fanatical nazi type makes up his mind to fight like hell, he is not a very nice opponent to have, though for sheer bravery I have never seen the like.

The tanks had not turned up 45 minutes after they had been promised, and in desperation the C.O. ordered the Carriers to see what they could do to help the beleaguered Company who were on their last legs. As they set off, the Shermans arrived and we sent them after to clinch matters, though as it happened, by the time they got there our excellent Carrier Platoon had turned the tide and the enemy were driven off with huge losses, and all our men (except the dead) were able to get back to their area. The sight of the tanks cheered them up and finished off the Bosche who withdrew all round, but leaving about 75 % casualties behind.

_____

(4)

It was dark by now and I must admit that we did not even stop to bury our dead - though a party was sent back the next day to give the appropriate crosses to the Scots.

Our little battle had finished the enemy for good, and the next day - we learnt later - our friends were able to advance over the next canal line unopposed.

All we were worried about was getting out before more trouble should start, and we were over that Bailey Bridge before very long, turning Eastwards as ordered towards a town called Beeringen.

Another short but bloody battle was over, and another field of crosses marks the spot.

_____

_____

— THE BREAKTHROUGH INTO HOLLAND —

PART V   THE BREAKTHROUGH INTO HOLLAND

(1)

Much has been written about the celebrated efforts of the 1st British Airborne Division in the famous battle of Arnhem, and the Official Account of this bloody affair is well worth reading. What I hope to do now is to give an account of some of the blood, sweat and toil suffered by the vanguard of the 2nd Army in trying to reach the gallant Air-men.

It was a most ambitious scheme, but should it prove 100% successful there was a good chance of the war with Germany being over.

Briefly, the plan was this. The Siegfried Line defences ended at the German/Dutch Border near Nijmegen and it was hoped by sheer speed of movement to outflank this and push into Germany before any remaining Bosche could get organised, and at the same time opening the way to liberating the whole of Holland and putting an end to the fly-bombs and V2's.

The Chief difficulty, as foreseen, would be the three great river barriers - Maas (Meuse), Waal and Lek (Lower Rhine). It was decided to cross these rivers at Grave, Nijmegen and Arnhem respectively, using large British and American Airborne forces to drop and secure these bridges before they could be blown up. It should be mentioned that at the moment the 2nd Army was held by considerable forces at the Meuse-Escaut canal south of Eindhoven, though they held a Bridgehead over the canal.

Three airborne (1st and 82 and 101 U.S.) Divisions set off from England on September 17th and the "DO" was on.

_____
(2)

We did not stay long at Beeringen (one day from what I remember) but moved forward to the Meuse Canal ready for the big effort. We parked down on a sandy stretch covered with low scrub, in the neighbourhood of Neerpelt, on the canal, where there was an untouched Bridge over which the bridgehead had already been made. The Guards Armoured Division were to be in the Van, with ourselves following immediately behind and it gave us a great feeling of security to be second string for once! We considered there would be a few days delay whilst the actual break-out from the small bridgehead was established, so we settled down and had as good a time as this uninteresting spot would allow. We even sent in to Diest, some miles back, and obtained several barrels of beer, and of course the usual scrounge for eggs went on. Two days doing nothing had come to seem like an absolute age and the most was made of it. Each dusk the bridgehead troops and the bridge itself were bombed and on the second evening there was considerably more activity and a quantity of anti-personnel bombs were dropped on us, though luckily without casualties. The next morning we were told to stand-by as the Guards had duly broken through and had now reached Eindhoven. There was only one order for the column - "forget everything except your accelerator, speed is vital".

---

(3)

Things did not work out quite as easily as that on the roads. The odd battle was going on in front, some vehicles broke down, Eindhoven was bombed at night and the road

blocked, and various other little causes meant
periodical stops. However, on the whole we
moved pretty steadily forward along the route
(see page 55) until Veghel, where the road was
lined with Yank Paratroops who had worked
their way back from Grave - the bridge there
was safely in our hands, without much
opposition - in order to line the axis. These
good fellows warned us that it would be
unwise to hang about as the Bosche were
closing in on the road; we heartily agreed at
once, and hurried on our way. And it was as
well we did, because we had scarcely gone
two hundred yards when the shelling started
just behind and we learned on arrival at
Nijmegen later in the day that the road had
been cut, and there had been great carnage.
Everyone on the spot was of course dragged
in, and A.A. Gunners and other specialists had
to get down and fight. The many "soft"
vehicles on the road were blown sky-high by
enemy tanks and guns, and what was more
important, we lost the battle and the forward
surge was checked. Actually, I had been in the
last vehicle to get through and the remainder
of the Battalion were lucky not to get caught in
the shambles. A hold-up further back saved
them this fate, but as it was, we did not see

them for two days, when the road was re-
opened. As things stood now, then, the
Guards were through complete (i.e. their
fighting units) and ¾^{ths} of our battalion was
through, and that is all. A bloody battle had
taken place for the great bridges at Nijmegen,
both some 400 yards long, and between the
Guards and the American Airborne lads they
were finally captured intact. So that was two
of the three objectives, and more or less up to
schedule, but with the further outlook very
unsettled whilst our one supply road was in
enemy hands. I should perhaps mention that a
British Corps (3 Divs.) was working up each
side of the road from the start point, clearing
things up for a good few miles either side. But
their progress was bound to be slow as they
were on foot and there was over 100 miles to
be done, with much opposition.

As the Bn. was now detached from the
rest of the Division, we were put under
command of the Guards temporarily, and they
ordered us to take over from the Americans
defending Nijmegen itself.

Nijmegen is a largish town, and a great centre of road and rail communications. It is only a few miles West of the German border, and in fact was one of the first towns to fall to the Bosche in the Battle of the Low Countries in 1940. Unfortunately the town was badly bombed in error by the Americans in - I think - 1943 and great damage had been done.

Nijmegen itself was pretty quiet now and we could hear battles raging ahead towards Arnhem about 8 miles away. Rumours came back that the Guards were not having a very happy time on what was known as "the Island" between the Lek and Waal Rivers. However, we had our work too cut out arranging our defences, to worry for the moment. All we could hope to do with our handful of troops was to take up positions covering the Road and Railway bridges, so vital to the future success of the operation; this we did.

When the rest of the Division were able to join us two days later we were relieved by 43rd Div and pushed on towards Arnhem. The shelling had gradually increased and now the bridges were under almost constant fire from big guns. We had to go on foot as the Island was not safe for soft vehicles. The limit of the advance by the Guards along the main road was at this stage Elst, a ruined village 3 miles on, and our job was to strike off East towards Bemmel to enlarge the bridgehead. Things were getting grim now. The 1st Airborne at Arnhem were in grave difficulties and our progress towards them was at a full stop, we hoped only temporarily. Unfortunately, two things - no, three - did not go to plan - 1. The enemy were in much greater strength and more organised than had been anticipated.

2. The physical lay-out was bad; the "Island" was very flat and completely overlooked from Arnhem (still in German hands), and the only roads were some yards above the rest of the ground. It was just suicide for tanks to get forward against the nests of 88 mm's.

3. Our main Axis Road from Belgium was "cut" as often as it was "through", and in any case Antwerp was not usable while the Bosche controlled the Delta from Walcheren, so that supply columns still had a terrific journey.

     In any case, the present failure to relieve the hard-pressed Air-men was certainly not the fault of the troops on the spot who had fought and were fighting with great valour and suffered large casualties. If the original Operation was to succeed, things would have to get moving pretty rapidly.

———————————————

——————————

————————

PART VI: STALEMATE AT ARNHEM, REICHWALD
(1)

As is well known, success did not crown the gallant efforts that had been made, but, by Heavens, the thing nearly came off. However, a miss is as good as a mile (or in this case 600 yards) so let us look for a moment at the credit side as the result of the Operation.

Casualties had been heavy on both sides, but the Allies could by now afford these more than the enemy. In addition we had pushed 150 miles into Holland and were now within a mile or so of Germany itself at the very top end of the Siegfried Line. Perhaps more important still, we had lessened the chances of the considerable forces in the coast areas escaping to Germany, and by drawing so many men and machines to this Sector, we had no doubt increased the prospects of an advance towards Germany all down the front from North to South.

It was about this time that we came to realise what a misnomer the word "Liberation" was. It signified more often than not a town or village laid in ruins with many civilian and

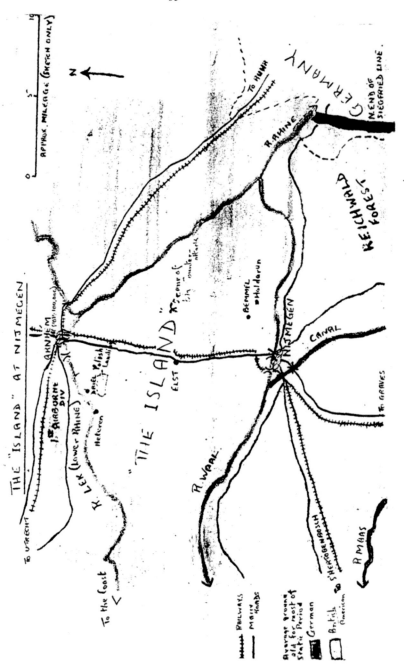

THE "ISLAND" AT NIJMEGEN

— TO FACE PAGE 46 —

APPROX. MILEAGE (SKETCH ONLY)

N

GERMANY

N END OF SIEGFRIED LINE.

TO HUNN

R. RHINE

REICHWALD FOREST

• BEMMEL
• Haldarun

General of 6th ounterattacks

NIJMEGEN

CANAL

TO GRAVES

ELST

ARNHEM

R. LEK (LOWER RHINE)

1ST AIRBORNE DIV

Poly Polish Landn

Heteren

"THE ISLAND"

R. WAAL

S'HERTOGENBOSCH

R. MAAS

TO UTRECHT

To the Coast

Railways
Main Roads
Average ground held for most of Static Period
German
British American

Allied casualties. As the great Captain Gus Mason, the Battalion wit throughout the whole war, put it - "You can go and bury Grannie now, Georges, we've been liberated!" The troops themselves, as was customary, summed things up pretty well, too. They had passed through the days of "Men England forgets" (M.E.F.), "Burma when Europe's finished"(B.W.E.F) and now the original interpretation of "B.L.A." - "Burma Looms Ahead" was unanimously changed to "B........r liberating anybody !"

As things turned out, the "liberated" area of the "Island" was to be our home for many a long week.

_____

(2)

Let us just pause to get ourselves in the picture as regards the lay-out of the Island. The map on page 65 shows that it is bounded on the North and East by the Upper Rhine, and South by the Waal, both rivers being a quarter of a mile wide and very deep and fast-flowing - formidable barriers even in modern warfare. To the West, the distance between the two rivers is only five miles, but a series of dykes, streams and canals completes the formation of the Island. We held, at this stage, less than a third of the area and were only in charge of a very small strip on the South bank of the Upper Rhine, made possible by a Polish Air-landing. The Island is flat and damp, with many ditches and canals, and the main foliage consists of fruit trees. East of Nijmegen but South of the Waal, is the large Reichwald Forest, also in German hands. Apart from the main Arnhem Road, the island is surrounded by a high "Bund" road, quite unusable as it was in full view of enemy guns. Gallant Poles and a Battalion of the Dorsets did manage to get contingents over near Driel to the far bank, but they had not the strength of Arms to save the Airborne men, and they suffered immense casualties. Finally it was decided to evacuate those air-men who remained and this was accomplished over a series of nights, with the help of the 43rd Division.

So what was the answer? To hang on to what we had, until another plan could be evolved.

It was now September 27th 1944, and Winter was very much in the offing; less than 4 months since "D" Day.

(3)

Well, of course it was Normandy all
over again. And very nice too!

The more the winter drew on, the less
cover from view was there from the trees, the
wetter the ground became, and the more
unpleasant was life. The enemy was very
offensive indeed, particularly as regards
shelling and mortaring and "a bad time was
had" by 50, 43 and 82 U.S. Airborne, which
three held our hard-won gains. Oh! and of
course the fine Guards Armoured who had
done so much in the push-through.

Battalions, Brigades and Divisions were
interchanged periodically to allow a very
occasional "holiday" in Nijmegen. A day or
so here and we longed to go back as the
shelling and bombing of the town were
incessant. There was the forward sector round
Driel, the centre sector forward of Elst, and
various areas on the East side around Bemmel
and Halderen, which latter villages were
captured with great difficulty. Food was good,
as there was much captured stuff, and plenty
of pigs and chickens running wild on the more

or less evacuated island. Running wild, yes
that is the expression. What does a pig do
when it runs wild? Having eaten several, we
discovered the answer, because the one we had
our eye on as the next victim, was found
devouring a complete German ... who had lain
there for some time! We stuck to chicken!
Sugar and jam were also very plentiful from a
jam factory near Elst. Wine was obtainable in
fair quantity, and the chart at Appendix 1 gives
a lay-out of our successes and failures in this
line from D Day onwards.

The long period of misery - almost 3
months - spent in this dreadful place is really
only the story told in Part 11 over again, so I
will confine myself to giving an account of
two events which particularly come to my
mind.

_____
(4)

"The crowning event of a magnificent
career" brought a personal visit from the Corps
Commander, a good chitty from Monty, and
eight newspaper reporters, to which latter we
gave an account as to what had happened. It
was like this.

We had heard rumours of a big Gerry breakthrough attempt almost as soon as we arrived for a spell in the sector between Elst and Bemmel, but as they were continually probing at us anyway, we were inclined to laugh it off, in which view we were supported by Brigade H.Q. who said we could consider the rumours as being quite without foundation. At this time things were very much the "thin red line" and the Bosche must have known this as (as we discovered afterwards) he decided to put all he had available into a narrow-front push in order - as his Order of the Day said - to finally re-take the Island and Nijmegen.

Piecemeal attacks had failed and he was changing the tactics.

It was early October, and at dusk one evening we noticed a rumbling in the distance but Brigade assured us it was nothing so we went about our business. I looked over to the Command Post we had dug that very day - we were normally in a house but decided it best to have a funk hole in case of trouble. The alternative telephone lines to the Post were in order and wireless aerials were ready in case of necessity. We had a meal, amidst increased rumbling - and further assurances from our superiors. "They're probably having a change-over, or perhaps clearing out altogether", they said, after consulting higher authority. We retired for the night, but as duty officer I did not sleep. After many hours of increased activity - one could almost pick out individual tanks moving about now, I decided at 0430 (stand-to was 0530) that in spite of any arguments, this was it. It was it.

I awoke the C.O. and told him my convictions and he at once ordered us to the dug post and we warned all Companies to stand-to. Just in time; within a matter of minutes all hell was let loose. The enemy appeared to have our whole area pin-pointed and mortaring and very big-calibre shelling descended on all positions. Our excellent telephone system lasted 5 seconds, and was then finished for good; to even attempt to mend the lines was futile and suicidal, as they had to all intents and purposes ceased to exist. All depended on Wireless and we were soon in touch with everyone by this means. So often our sets were excellent until shelling started only to be useless through interference at the crucial time. Today they stood by us, and

saved all our lives. Why? Our only hope as
the battle progressed was found - as so often -
to be artillery support. The guns were there in
large quantities, this we had been told as soon
as we had flashed back the news. But they had
to be brought to bear on the right spot at the
right time and this was entirely dependant on
communications, and quick transmission of
messages; a target might only be in a spot for
minutes, or seconds.

The bad news began to come through
from Companies. We are surrounded by 10
tanks.... our forward platoon has been overrun
... hundreds of Bosche are lining up in the
wood in front.... we have brewed up two
Tigers, but 12 more are coming on ... we have
only 20 left now and cannot hold out ... all the
anti-tank guns are knocked out, can we pull
back? ... and so on. Each time the news was
flashed to Brigade and to our gunner friend
with his wireless in the next hole in the
ground. Within an unbelievably short time
down came the barrage, and as it fell so came
the corrections from Coys., when necessary.
The gunners - 124 Field and many others -
were magnificent and attack after attack was
broken up by this means, and hour after hour

the battle raged on. We pleaded for help, which was promised but not forthcoming, and the Companies dwindled down in most cases to a handful. The tanks (we had none with us) had begun to wonder; 9 were knocked before our guns became defunct and they probably thought they were up against an anti-tank screen, which was not the case ... any longer.

Still hordes of "grey-jackets" formed up for the big push and each time they were brought under a murderous barrage. The enemy shelling began to ease off about dusk, but we were still very worried as naturally by this time the Battalion was fit for very little and no relief had arrived. In addition, for about the first time ever we had been 24 hours without food - movement forward was quite impossible. About 2000 Hrs. the enemy broke and ran all round and as this happened our relief arrived. We had lost many, many good officers and men, and 250 yds of ground. But the island was secure and the enemy had lost at least 12 tanks and probably thousands of men - over four hundred were found dead in one field alone cut to shreds by our artillery. We got out as quickly as we could stagger, leaving our newcomers in charge and went back half a mile to flop down in exhaustion for the night, feeling how lucky we were to be alive.

When we learned the next day that our narrow front had been attacked by 3 Panzer Divisions we had a bit of a shock! Our bomb-happy remnants were taken to Nijmegen (of all places!) for a "rest".

Thank you, Gunners!

---
(5)

The other incident that I have felt worth recording from this static period occurred forward of Bemmel in early November.

There was a "fly-over" bridge over an arterial road under construction, which was suspected of being an enemy observation post. It was carefully watched for four days and no sign of movement was seen, so assuming it to be unoccupied we were ordered to take it over. Our beloved Germans had boxed pretty cleverly, and sure enough the platoon approaching it were heavily fired on, losing an Officer and sergeant, the remainder withdrawing. It was still thought that the fire came from somewhere covering the bridge, so two stretcher-bearers bravely volunteered to go and find the casualties under cover of a Red Cross flag. Unfortunately the Company Commander insisted upon going too in spite of protests from the medical men that he was not protected by the flag.

As the small party approached the bridge - unopposed - an S.S. Officer popped his head from a dug-out in the neighbourhood of the bridge and "invited" our friends in. They had been there, cunningly concealed, all the time! How do I know? I will tell you.

The S.S. Officer, believe it or not, was a gentleman. He rightly kept our Officer (who remarked suavely as though one of the famous "Two Types" - "Oh dear! how annoying") and told the S.B.s that the other officer had been taken off as a prisoner and the Sergeant's body was there for the taking. He even showed them round the post (and the information gathered proved most useful) and then said they were free to return.

He must have been the exception which proves the rule about S.S. troops!

(6)

And so the time dragged on in misery with a spell in the Driel sector and a long one of three weeks in a flood-ridden Halderen sector, until we finally learned that in view of the lack of reinforcements our Division was to be pulled out and used to bolster up the other dwindling Divisions. To preserve the name we had made, a small cadre was to be sent home. Who would be lucky?

PART VII   GOODBYE, MR. EUROPE.
(1)

The last few days on the "Island" were sheer misery. Would we survive, or "get one" at the eleventh hour? Who would get home, and who flung in somewhere else? Then there was the added fear of the blowing of the dykes by the Germans, to flood The Island, an Operation which was to be followed by an Allied evacuation - no doubt accompanied by massed shelling of the one remaining bridge (the railway crossing having been some time previously blown sky-high by the celebrated German frogmen, in a most courageous exploit).

However, luck was with us, and we pulled out in early December, one day before the expected flooding came, and made our way to Roulers (shades of World War I) in Belgium, preparatory to the great break-up.

We lucky "old stagers" were mad with excitement at going home, whilst the unlucky newer-comers were of course very despondent at having to change units, though they were in most cases to receive some home leave first.

---

(2)

A great time was had in the peace of Roulers and finally - just in time for Christmas - the active career of the 7th Battalion, the Green Howards was brought to an end as we remnants embarked for the Mother Country, tired but triumphant!

-THE END-

56

— APPENDIX ONE —

CARTE DES VINS JUNE 6 — DEC 15, 1944.

PLACE	TYPE (S)	QUANTITY	PRICE	REMARKS.
Normandy	Rough Cider.	Small	Free	████ Dreadful.
..	Calvados (Distilled Cider)	..	Soap or Bully Beef.	Undrinkable (45% Alc. and caused one death)
France and Belgium (If first in Town)	Everything	Good.	Free.	Liberation Celibrations
France and Belgium (After liberation)	NONE.	—	—	Except very watery coloured stuff called bière or something!
Holland.	Beer	Small	6ᵈ half pint.	Poor stuff.
..	Bols (Gin)	Large, for a time.	Loot.	Excellent.
..	Cointreau.	Small.	£3 Bot.!	.. if dear
..	French Wines.	Fair	10/- - 15/- Bot.	.. .. ..
..	Issue Spirits.	Poor.	3/6 Bot!	Nice work if you could get it.

57.

APPENDIX TWO..

"That Will Be The Day, Cads"
a song written by the author, with apologies to the WESTERN
BROTHERS, to illustrate the frame of mind of the Infantry
towards the close of the Normandy campaign.

o————————o

When 50 Div. is in reserve, —
　　That'll be the day, cads, that'll be the day!
When we all get what we deserve, —
　　That'll be the day, cads, that'll be the day!
The mail will come within a day,
There'll be no longing for the fray,
It won't come yet so till that day —
　　It's "fling 'em in again, Cads, fling 'em in".

When Monty says "I'll take them out" —
　　That'll be etc.
And our reply is "Wilco, out① " —
　　That'll be etc.
The news will fill us all with smiles,
Especially after all our trials,
And even if we've all got piles!
　　Fling us in again, Cads, fling us in.

When "Road Clear"② means there are no mines —
　　That'll be etc.
When Pronto's③ finished laying lines —
　　That'll be etc.

1. A Wireless expression meaning "Message Understood, I will act on it".
2. Often roads were declared "clear of mines, only for some poor devil to go up sky-high.
3. Pronto: Wireless code for Signals Officer.

The end, they say, is now in sight,
The Hun has felt the Allies' might.
So let the Yanks through under Dwight —
    fling 'em in etc.

When Haricot Oxtail[4] has no bones —
    That'll be etc.
When Villers Bocage[5] is cleared of stones —
    That'll be etc.
Our gang is always in the front,
In every battle bears the brunt,
But when we ask if we may shunt —
    It's "fling 'em in again, cads, fling 'em in."

When Adolf's hordes are all in jug —
    That'll be etc.
When B.H.Q. need not be dug —
    That'll be etc.
The Russians hurry day by day,
Towards the land of Bosch at bay,
There's still snow on their boots, they say.
    So fling 'em in etc.

When "two days' rest"[6] means two days rest —
    That'll be etc.
When the M.T.O. can pass his test —
    That'll be etc.
We've been to lands of eggs and bread[7].

4. A tinned food full of queer shaped bones.
5. Razed to the ground by R.A.F.
6. A rest seldom was one, owing to reorganisation.
7. Egypt — where everyone sells eggs and bread.

59.

We've learned to like our biddy red[8]
And still we bury German dead —
Fling us in again etc.

When the Brigadier turns up on time[9] —
That'll be etc.
And sees our drill and says "that's fine" —
That'll be etc
We've often heard this "fling 'em in",
And always say "we've been flung in",
But still they say above the din —
"Fling 'em in again, lads, fling 'em in

_____

8. Red biddy — Sicilian Red wine.
9. Ours seldom was on time.